EVL.. .. ..AM

Sylvia E. Walker

ARTHUR H. STOCKWELL LTD.
Elms Court   Ilfracombe   Devon
Established 1898

British Library Cataloguing-in-Publication Data.
A catalogue record for this book is available
from the British Library.

ISBN 0 7223 3218-1
Printed in Great Britain by
Arthur H. Stockwell Ltd.
Elms Court   Ilfracombe
Devon

*This book is dedicated to the memory
of my mother and father, also to my
sister Hazel, family and friends.*

Be still, sad heart! and cease repining;
Behind the clouds is the sun still shining;
Thy fate is the common fate of all,
Into each life some rain must fall.

Henry Wadsworth Longfellow.

Contents

Introduction

A gifted author was asked how he was motivated to write his books. He recalled a friend's advice, that if he had something to say, he should write about it. He knew of many true stories which could touch the hearts of his readers.

Writing books and articles is easier said than done. Established writers, past and present, deserve our admiration and respect. My own small attempt has heightened my awareness of their achievements. I do not have the imagination for inventing fictitious stories, so I am writing the only story I know, that of family life.

I was fortunate to be deeply loved by my parents. Regardless of ups and downs, I always felt completely safe in their presence. To the outside world, they were just an ordinary, hard-working couple, but to me, they were moulded from 'uncommon clay', and were the salt of the earth.

Nursing my mother and father in their hour of need was a privilege, not a duty.

From Yorkshire to Lancashire

January 2nd, 1959, had arrived at last. I had just left behind my first Grammar School in the West Riding of Yorkshire, and I was sixteen years old. My parents, younger sister Anna and myself were abandoning one county for another, or so we had been told, as we travelled across the Pennine moors, to the seaside town of Coverton, on Lancashire's west coast.

The linking motorway was still a distant dream, and so it was that we were crammed amongst the furniture in the back of an old removal van, as it bumped its way up and down the winding roads. I remember being wedged on a tiny stool, half buried under the piano, and fervently praying that I would not bang my head. Completing the scene was our stray cat, Blackie, who was so bewildered by events, that when the van driver halted at a transport cafe, flew like a flash of lightning, down the road and across a field. Mercifully, Anna's agility and quick wits saved the day, and following endless manoeuvres, Blackie was safely secured in the top drawer of the dressing table.

Regrettably, better transport was out of the question at this time, since my parents had committed most of their savings towards the purchase of our second home. This house also would have been too expensive, had we not found it in such a derelict state. It had been empty for two years, following the deaths of its former occupants; three elderly sisters.

My father was a plasterer and builder by trade, as were his father and grandfather. Being an eternal optimist, he anticipated that he would be able to transform our new home into a meritorious condition.

Despite this new beginning at Coverton, experience shows, that links with our early, impressionable years are never completely severed. We sometimes believe that we can escape from events in our past, and bury whatever we conveniently wish to forget, but reality is far more complex than the human mind can possibly imagine. Life's road cannot be divided into clearly defined areas, black and white. Instead, there are infinite shades of grey, each making its own contribution.

To complete the picture, I will first take a step backwards and share some of the experiences of my young life in Yorkshire, after the Second World War.

Childhood Memories

One day, when playing with my toys, I discovered a strange object; a gas mask, abandoned at the bottom of a cupboard during the war. Apparently, a temporary air-raid shelter had been constructed for the people living in our road. Although this shelter was never used, the surrounding cities, with their engineering works and munitions factories, were badly bombed. Such was my first, fleeting knowledge of a war-torn world.

A very special first-birthday gift, was my dog Spot. Spot was a white mongrel with a large, black spot on his back, and hence his name. Spot's main failing was to romp with the cows in the field which verged alongside the back garden. The ghastly smell which ensued meant that my parents were constantly trying to wash him clean. Spot hated this ritual, but he would never learn to behave himself.

On one memorable occasion, when Spot had enjoyed his usual rendezvous with the cows, he was not content to stay at home, and unknown to a soul, not only found his way to my Junior School, but somehow began wandering round the classrooms. What a commotion!

All of a sudden, the headmaster marched into my room, holding his nose as he dragged dirty Spot by the collar, and then bellowed, "Whose dreadful dog is this?"

With broken heart and with Spot in tow, I trudged home, mortified and humiliated by the whole episode. Needless to say that my disgrace of a dog was blissfully unaware of all the havoc he had caused, wagging his tail merrily and enjoying all the fuss.

In theory, our home in Yorkshire was supposed to have a garden both back and front, but in practice, the story was very different. All other gardens in the road were kept meticulously tidy; one of the reasons being that the children living nearby used our garden for their playground. The grass in the front garden grew so long that this area became a children's paradise — a perfect place to play hide-and-seek.

My parents attempted to grow potatoes and cabbages in the back garden, but of greater importance to the younger generation, was their acquisition of some chickens and two beloved rabbits, Whisky and Bobtail.

It was indeed a tragic day for our neighbour, Mrs Wiggett, when a cow crashed through the back fence, trampled all over her precious flower borders, and then had the audacity to poke its head through her kitchen window, just as she was washing the dishes. The traumas which followed were never to be forgotten by anyone within hearing distance. To think that our wilderness of a garden remained untouched!

One of my treasured delights in the warmer weather was playing with friends at acting and 'dressing-up' in all the old cast-offs we could muster. An important occasion was when we performed a wedding, and rolled a long piece of shabby stair carpet from the front door, down the garden path to the gate. Long were the arguments deciding who would play the coveted roles of bride and groom, although the minister was considered to be the most important person, possibly because he took so long reading his profound words from our battered Common Prayer book. Anna often became justifiably disgruntled, because, being smaller than the rest, she was always relegated to the rank of bridesmaid.

Bonfire Night brought its own particular brand of excitement. How

we trailed backwards and forwards along the winding road leading to the wood, pulling down branches, only to lose many of them on the way home.

Such boundless energy also manifested itself when the snow finally arrived, with the usual snowball fights and toboggan rides in the hills nearby.

My father was involved with an Undenominational Sunday School, which Anna and I attended each Sunday morning and afternoon. My mother was a member of the Methodist Church, and often we supported her at the Evening Service, when she sang in her deep contralto voice, from the front choir stalls. My lasting impression of these peaceful evenings was of the sun, sending its dying rays to illuminate the stained-glass windows for a final time, as we said our prayers while the birds twittered on the rooftop.

Finally, our souls were lifted to a higher dimension, as the organ music swelled and the choir and congregation joined in the final hymn.

As the years unfolded, little sadnesses occurred, particularly in the mind of a child. Whisky and Bobtail escaped from their rabbit hutch, never to return. The chickens steadily decreased in number as they graced the dining table for many a Sunday lunch. Far worse was the time when Spot developed an incurable disease in his feet, and my father took him for his final visit to the vet. I cried myself to sleep for many weeks, asking Jesus to take care of Spot until I saw him again in heaven. Then I would wash him for ever and ever.

Such were my halcyon days, untroubled and unfettered. Life was filled with simple pleasures and was so much happier for them.

The Middle Years

I imagine that for many people, memory and age are inversely proportional. I remember so vividly the happenings of my younger years compared, say, with the happenings of a week or so ago, or alternatively, with the items on my last shopping list, when I arrived at the shops without it. This theory possibly explains why so many memories of my Grammar School teachers persist clearly in the mind.

The most compelling was my Mathematics teacher, Miss Ironside, noted for her strong Geordie accent and sarcastic comments. The class could hear a pin drop when she walked into the room and stood by her desk on the dais, gloating down upon us. She seemed to spend most of her time sharpening red crayons over the wastepaper basket, in order to place either huge ticks or crosses all over our books. Two examples of a particular topic were written on the blackboard and the explanation was complete. If you dared to question, you felt a halfwit. Her reply to every question was the same, "My dear girl, it's as easy as falling off a log!"

The Geography teacher, Miss Shilling, caused most amusement with her permanent affliction of rapid blinking. My friend and I spent many lessons counting the number of blinks and comparing our scores. A love of Geography never had the chance to blossom.

How the pupils sighed, green with envy, when the attractive PE Mistress became engaged to the Science Master; and what a catastrophe when the engagement abruptly ended a few months later. The reason for this disaster was the subject of intense speculation, and rumour persisted that this master ended the romance because his fiancée spent too much of their savings. Sad to say, both teachers left school shortly afterwards and no longer could their liaison, or the lack of it, be the priority on our gossip agenda.

It is fair to say that the PE Mistress set particularly high standards, both for herself and her pupils. She always made a similar comment on my school report, to the effect that although I did not achieve very much, I always tried my best. The truth was that I never achieved anything at all.

In one impulsive act of bravado, I volunteered to enter the High Jump for my 'House' on Sports Day. The following two weeks were wretched, as I constantly prayed to be relieved of this self-inflicted burden. Lo and behold, my prayers were answered, although not in the manner I had imagined. At the eleventh hour, I tripped and sprained my ankle. Bandages were applied thickly as ample evidence of the mishap, and some unsuspecting soul became the replacement. A sprain has never been so warmly welcomed.

Each Form usually has a spokesperson in its ranks; someone whom the rest can rely on to speak up for them, who will dare to venture where others fear to tread. Such a person was my friend, Rosamund. One particular School Open Day, she persuaded a group of us to sing a selection from 'The Desert Song'. The musical entertainment proved short-lived however, when we collapsed in helpless giggles during her special solo 'Blue Heaven and You and I . . . .' Her facial contortions had to be seen to be believed. Even many in the audience endeavoured to hide their amusement behind handkerchiefs or wide-brimmed hats.

Rosamund also took it upon herself to include the whole Form in a production of 'Macbeth', which would be performed for the School Play Competition. There are no prizes for guessing who played Macbeth. Thankfully, I escaped quite lightly, as one of the three witches.

The one activity which spanned a number of my younger years, was that of learning to play the piano. I have often regretted abandoning the private lessons which my parents could barely afford, as school examinations loomed ever larger as a time-consuming priority.

On reflection, however, there were other factors to consider. My music teacher was an elderly gentleman, and his devoted wife used to bring him his glass of medicine during my piano lessons. The medicine may have been a panacea for his constitution, but it certainly had a dreadful odour. As he heaved deeply beside me at the piano, the aroma would ruin my powers of concentration, causing many a wrong note to be played. Sadly, it became evident that the gentleman was unwell, but he loved his music and cared about his pupils.

It is sufficient to say, that shortly after these lessons ended, the gentleman died and a few months later, his broken-hearted wife followed him to his resting place. Many years would pass before I learned that his name lived on for posterity, because I accidentally discovered it in the 'Songs Of Praise' hymn book.

My first term in the Sixth Form would also be the last at my Yorkshire Grammar School. In the summer of 1958, during a family holiday in Coverton, my parents came upon the large, Victorian house near the sea, which was about to become the family home for the next twenty-five years. Both in their late forties, they had been reflecting long and hard about whether or not they should remain living in the same place for the rest of their lives; no mean consideration in the mid-twentieth century. The opportunity for a new beginning presented itself in the form of this dilapidated house and they grasped it with both hands. My father would work for a building firm, my mother would contribute to finances by taking paying guests in the holidays and Anna and I would be transferred to a local school.

Thus the stage was set. After goodbyes to relatives and friends, we ventured into the unknown in the New Year of 1959, into unforeseeable circumstances and events which would shape the destinies of us all. We remembered the past with affection, but more importantly, we looked to the future with both optimism and trepidation.

Life at Coverton

Our second home had no distinguishing features, except that it stretched a deceptively long way from front to back. There were two large attics on the third floor and anyone who was tall enough, could peer out of the front attic window, to view the sand hills and sea beyond.

It is difficult to describe all the work which needed doing when the property was inspected at close quarters. Old, cracked, nineteenth-century fireplaces abounded in most rooms. All woodwork was covered with a semblance of thick, dark treacle. In fact, the overall picture could be summarised as being broodingly Dickensian, as if one had been transported by the time machine to a bygone age. Any remaining days of the school Christmas holiday were spent scraping off numerous layers of wallpaper everywhere.

Until Easter, the house was inundated with various workmen; people whom my father had encountered during the daily round. The decorator was a particularly fortunate fellow, scaling the dizzy heights from a long period of unemployment to months of solid, hard work. With zealous enthusiasm, he became quite carried away by his efforts, signing his name with a flourish, 'Jack the Lad', on every wall he encountered.

How well I remember the electrician with his carrot-coloured, curly hair and moonbeam face, juggling with endless coils of wire near my feet, as I struggled with homework on a wobbly desk, losing the fight with my concentration.

My father's spare time was mainly spent removing the fireplaces, then bricking up and plastering the holes. One evening, I found him up a ladder in the kitchen, his head invisible because it was stuck through a gaping hole in the ceiling. Dust and rubble were everywhere. I thought it wise to bid a hasty retreat when my shocked gaze focused on my mother's pale, anxious face.

Many more years would pass before I learned how desperately lonely my mother had been during our earliest years at Coverton, and how she used to stand on the railway bridge, gazing longingly at the trains as they disappeared into the distance, in the direction of Yorkshire. Youth, by its very nature, is oblivious of such finer feelings.

Another ordeal, alien to her proud nature, was that of taking her children to second-hand shops, searching for cheap, yet suitable furniture which would complement our own sparse collection, and help to fill the numerous empty rooms.

Intensive preparations were concluded by Good Friday when our first paying guests arrived, complete with extra woollen blankets and water bottles. They were leaving nothing to chance.

The weeks passed, and in contrast to the bitterly cold winter months, our first Coverton summer proved to be one of the hottest on record. To think that we did not yet possess either a fridge or a vacuum cleaner!

The daily routine saw Anna speeding to the shops on her bicycle whilst I plodded through the cleaning, aided by brush, shovel, polish and duster, and Mother prepared and cooked the meals.

Many people enjoy the challenge of organising guest houses and hotels. Unfortunately for my family, this work proved to be a soul-destroying operation, which for myself, has left its mark to this day. My mother, inexperienced in such matters, did not charge paying guests enough money and people took advantage of her generosity. Those who were sufficiently magnanimous to offer more, were few indeed. No wonder that any welcome offered to friends grew out of all proportion into a worrying ordeal, rather than a normal pleasure.

Guests were to come and go for about five years, mainly during the school summer holiday weeks, when Anna and I could offer help.

Any such worries were further compounded on the day my father lost his job. I never fully understood the reason for this, but maybe because he was one of the last men to be employed by the building firm, he was also one of the first to leave. The distressing fact remained, that for the first time in his life, my father had no work.

This problem proved to be a mixed blessing. On a positive note, he began helping local people repair their properties, often replacing slates which had been blown off rooftops by the gales, or trying to cure eternal 'damp' problems. Such work resulted in him starting his own small business.

At last he was his own master; self-employed, with his very own bill headings. His pride and self-esteem were restored. My mother had worked in an office on leaving school, specialising in book-keeping, so she was able to balance the books.

Regrettably, there was a downside to these promising plans. My father was no businessman and never took the longer view. He just lived from week to week and never worried about the next. It was left to my mother to try and save money from the bills which had been paid and to worry about queries over the ones which were still owing. She used to dread answering the door bell, only to be confronted by would-be irate customers. They were angry that my father had promised to call and inspect repair work, but had never appeared. Such matters inevitably led to bitter arguments between my parents and these in turn formed my unhappiest memories during the early Coverton years. The saddest fact was that these arguments, the futile claims and counter claims, were so unnecessary. If only my father had been more methodical and organised . . . . . If only he had recorded people's requests in the order they had been received and then worked steadily through his lists . . . . . If only he had kept his promises to customers instead of forgetting them . . . . . He meant well. He was a good, kind man, but you cannot be all things to all men. No one can.

In retrospect, this was the first time in my life that I witnessed a clash of personalities; a complete incompatibility of character. I was too young to be consciously aware of this at the time, but only too aware of the heartache such problems could unleash.

Ironically, the most peaceful time in my parents' life together, came many years later when my father was dying from a long cancer illness, shortly before he reached retirement age. Sadly, the twilight of their shared years was cruelly cut short. The earlier years could not be relived and righted. What a waste!

Endings and Beginnings

My school years soon came to an end at Coverton. I was now in the Sixth Form studying Advanced Level subjects; the academic standard being higher than that of my first Grammar School. This meant that not only was I learning new work with my peers, but also trying to understand and learn any work I had missed.

One able companion at school, a near neighbour, was my Polish friend. She had been rescued by relatives from certain death when her parents perished in the Holocaust. She never knew her birthday, only that she was born in the middle of March, 1942. Each day after school, we walked home together and spent most of the time discussing our work. I hung on to her every word, hoping to be given clues about how to do my homework. I must confess that as soon as school was out of sight, I also removed the regulation Panama hat in the hope of receiving a smile from the boy with black, curly hair, who worked at the local garage.

Every spare moment was given to school work. The staff were generous with their time, giving me extra help, so the least I could do was to try and repay their encouragement in the only way I knew. Mercifully, I was eventually rewarded with pleasing examination results, a testament to good teaching and hard work.

Maybe because I was 'dragging my feet' at school, feeling inferior to friends, or maybe because I had always lacked self-confidence, but I firmly believed that I was not of University standard and no one told me differently. I also hoped to become a teacher, and thus applied to enter Training College. I was rejected by a college in the South of England, but accepted by a new college in the Midlands. Here, I would spend the next three years of my life, learning as much about myself, as about my subjects and chosen career.

Lessons to be Learned

It is a sad fact of life, that we can be in the company of others, yet still feel isolated. The mask we wear for the outside world can convey such a different impression to the real human being. I first experienced the truth of these statements at college, away from the sheltered environment of home, but they have been reinforced many times in later years.

What gifted actors and actresses many of us become for many reasons. We can pretend so many things. We may pretend we are happy, at peace with ourselves and the world, when the reality can be constant, inner turmoil. In particular, we may pretend in the cause of peace, when we are attacked with a cruel, unthinking tongue and are belittled. The spoken word is a potent weapon. It can pierce like a dagger and cannot be retracted. Our self-esteem may be in tatters and our confidence shattered, but no one knows. Pretence abounds in all manner of guises, but the day can come when the 'worm turns' and honesty begins. Life may be more painful and friends may be lost, but at least we are true to ourselves, a quality of character to be treasured.

My own 'moment of truth' came with the failure of my marriage. When college ended in 1963, I began teaching at a local Grammar School. The following summer, at my sister's wedding, I was introduced to the best man, my future husband. He was a tall, handsome person, with a charming smile and winning ways. I believed he was all the things I had hoped for in a partner; upright and honest, thoughtful and kind, strong in character but gentle in manner. For my part, there was unquestioning affection. The immortal words of Elizabeth Barrett Browning said it all. I loved him 'to the depth, breadth and height my soul could reach, and with the breath, smiles, tears of all my life'. He was the beginning and end of my world. I felt truly blessed.

Six years after first meeting my husband, our marriage had ended and tragically, by this time, I was incapable of feeling anything. Negative emotions, such as anger and hurt, no longer existed. There was simply a numbness, an ocean of emptiness, a desolation that I could never have fully understood, had it not happened to me. It was as if my soul, the core of my being, no longer existed and only an empty shell remained.

So much could be written about the intervening years, a roller-coaster ride of every emotion imaginable, but this is wiser left unsaid. Old wounds from the past should not be allowed to fester and taint the future. Instead, we must try and believe that however desperately sad our situation, some good must come out of it.

I am reminded of the writer, Celia Haddon's words, 'I do not believe that unhappiness in itself can be good for anybody. Yet sometimes inner change emerges after emotional pain, and at a time of unhappiness there is some comfort in remembering this'.

I only know that I emerged from the darkness a changed person, albeit unconsciously. I became more resilient and hopefully a better, more compassionate human being. Never again would I condemn anyone for anything without knowing the full facts of the story. This rarely happens. Never again would I knowingly hurt or upset anyone. Unfortunately, kindness is often mistaken for weakness, so it is important that we are careful and learn where to draw the line in difficult situations. My whole attitude to everything I encountered, took on a different meaning. I also knew that whatever else life threw at me, nothing could be sadder or more difficult to face than the preceding few years.

Yes, I had changed. I now belonged to life's crisis copers and could stand alone. At last my priorities were in the right order. I was alive and well. The sun was emerging from behind the clouds and the future beckoned, but twenty-five more years would pass before I felt completely whole again. Only then would the sun be at its brightest.

The Aftermath

My lasting legacy from these turbulent years has been impaired hearing. The problem only became apparent when I had completed further studies at University and had begun teaching again. The nerves of the inner ear, in both ears, were affected. An operation might have resulted in complete deafness; a risk I dare not take. So with the support of friends, and wearing hearing aids, I persevered with my work. Any private worries concerning this difficulty had to be swiftly cast aside because of more pressing family problems.

In 1974, my mother suffered a nervous breakdown and different contributory factors became evident. There were problems associated with my father's business, the worries my married life had caused and not least, the departure of my sister and her young family to begin a new life in North America; each had taken its toll and there was a price to pay. The search for effective medication seemed endless, but gradually the shattered pieces fitted together again, rather like a jigsaw puzzle, and recovery was slow but sure. This progress would also have been complete, had not my father's cancer illness cruelly intervened.

The care and attention my father needed, meant that my mother had little time to dwell on her own illness. His welfare and comfort mattered above all else. The lounge became his bedroom, and his bed was placed by the window. Until his sight deteriorated, he could see the garden and road beyond. The nurses visited daily for eight months, until he died peacefully in his sleep, on April 21st, 1977.

That same night, I was resting in a small camp bed at the side of my father's bed, when suddenly, there seemed to be movement throughout the darkened room. There was a presence, intangible but very real. My father's spirit was going to heaven. The stillness descended again and I knew he had died.

Changing Scenes

When I returned to teaching, I had been unable to obtain a suitable post locally and was now working at a school in the heart of Lancashire, approximately one hour's car journey from Coverton. I was also the proud owner of my own small bungalow.

The few years following my father's death passed quietly. The only problem on the horizon was the condition of my mother's house, which was badly in need of repair. Her state pension was her only source of income and was needed for basic necessities. The only way I could raise sufficient money was by selling my bungalow. The bungalow was too small for my mother to live there too, but regardless of its size, she did not wish to leave her friends and familiar surroundings. Most important of all, neither of us wanted to lose the family home at Coverton. For all these reasons, I took a chance and sold my bungalow, using most of the revenue to finance home improvements.

I also travelled daily between school and home for three years, while I tried to find work in the Coverton area. Unfortunately, good teaching posts comparable to my present work were at a premium and I was unsuccessful. The travelling could not continue indefinitely and eventually I admitted defeat. My mother was also growing older and needed more care. We both reached the inevitable conclusion that the Coverton house must be sold. The proceeds were used to buy another bungalow, quite near the first and only three miles from school.

Life was getting on to an even keel once again, when my mother began to lose weight. Her throat was badly swollen and she had difficult eating. She was found to have cancer of the throat and lungs and died at home on March 21st, 1990. She was brought back to Coverton, her spiritual home, for burial.

In Heavenly Love Abiding

"Death cannot kill what never dies." *William Penn.*

I have often thought that the manner in which my parents dealt with their cancer illnesses, epitomised their characters. My father faced the inevitable with a quiet, bewildered resignation, but my mother, with her stubborn streak and true northern grit, fought to the bitter end. I will never forget the last time she tried to raise her head from the pillow, but failed. Her strength had gone. Her last words to me were, "God Bless You".

Months later, when I was looking through my mother's belongings, I came across her writing in an old diary. She wrote, *'If you are fated to have someone old in your care, cherish and love them, even if you have to drag the love from your toe ends. Old people can be churlish and awkward. They can find it difficult to fit in with the technological age and sometimes mistakenly think they know best. Do not forget that the elderly have much to remember. Two world wars, the depression of the thirties and the struggle to get to work before the age of motor transport, are but a few memories. When you sometimes feel despondent after helping an older person each day, try and show them gratitude for all they have done for you. When their time comes to go, get down on your knees and thank God for giving you the strength and patience to do your lovable best for someone you will never see again. In return, God will bless you and give you the peace in your heart that you have never known before.'*

Yes, I have been blessed and peace has come, but it has taken its own time.

It seems fitting that my final tribute should be a poem, the only poem my mother attempted to write. The words convey the humour and spirit of life and not the sadness of death. I hope this poem will raise a smile. Here we are given a glimpse of the 'real Mum', the practical homemaker. I believe this is how she would wish to be remembered.

The Fireplace Saga

My daughter and I decided one day
A new fireplace to have without further delay.
The one that was there, was old and decayed
For twenty long years it had been such a treasure,
Giving much warmth and comfort in moments of leisure.

We went to the shop, paid our money and placed
An order for fireplace which looked nice to the gaze.
The man said he'd come the very next day.
This was a surprise and caused us dismay
For the room must be emptied, Oh! what an upset
We ne'er dreamed how such a hard task could be met.

We struggled and lifted and pushed and we carried
Chairs, table and rug, had since I was married.
The piano was stubborn and wouldn't answer the call,
So we dragged out the carpet, underlay and all.

The workman arrived with hammer and chisel
And knocked out the old fireplace as clean as a whistle.
He filled most of the hole with bricks and cement,
Put in the new fireplace and then off he went.

My heart sank to my shoes as I looked at the soot,
Which in every conceivable place had found root.
My friend offered help, but I said, 'You go home
And I'll come to tell you when I have done.'

I lost count of the buckets of water I carried
Backwards and forwards, with tired arms and feet.
I finally scrubbed the last inch of the floorboard
Feeling tired and discouraged and thoroughly beat.

My Prayer

Now, when I die and go up to heaven,
I earnestly pray that the furniture's fitted,
The pianos have wings and the carpets are stuck to the floor.
That the windows self-clean, and the paintwork so shines
As if angels had come through the door
With dusters and polish, and hung up clean curtains.
No one could pray for much more.

But if prayers are not answered and spring-cleaning I spy,
I will spread out my wings and back to earth I will fly.

So if when you're shopping, you see a strange vision
Of someone passing by in bedraggled condition,
It will only be me in despair at my plan,
Who has come back to earth to collect my dustpan.

Strength for Today and Bright Hope for Tomorrow

It is He who had made the night a mantle for you and sleep a rest. He makes each day a resurrection. *The Koran.*

Following my mother's death, I continued teaching for three more years, until 1993. My hearing problems had grown into an unequal struggle over the years and following hospital tests, I was granted early retirement. When the bungalow had been sold, I returned to live at Coverton, near my old home and near the sea.

Sadly, at present, I am fighting a personal battle, that of breast cancer. The doctors and nurses gave freely of the their loving care when I entered hospital for my mastectomy operation. Constant support was also offered by my sister, Anna, who journeyed from her American home to encourage and support in time of need. The help I gave our mother and father has, in turn, been given to me. No one could ask for more.

Each night, at bedtime, I go down on my knees, thanking God for helping me through the day and asking Him to guide me through the morrow. Yes, time is remorseless, but remembrance is eternal.

With Gratitude

Look backward with gratitude
Look onward with hope
Look upward with confidence.
Author Unknown.

There is one last task left for me to accomplish, a tribute to the people whose lives have touched mine, who have helped to make me what I am and have brought me to this day:

To Hazel. There was a time when we could have so easily drifted apart. Thank you for 'hanging on in there' and guiding me along the rocky paths. I love you.

To my bright Chicago lights; Dixie Lee and Stephen, Susan and Keith, and Andrew our twinkling star. May the lights never dim.

To Sydney, for working hard and giving a wonderful life to Hazel and the family in the United States of America. Their future is secure and my mind is at rest.

To Sydney's parents, Rhoda and George Horsfield, and sister, Margaret, for their support.

To American friends who have welcomed me with open arms.
To Sheila and Peter, Bonnie and George, Barbara and George, Julie and Kerris, and Connie.
To Chris Chytraus who founded 'The Sharing Place' in Salt Lake City. The Sharing Place provides a caring environment where children, young people and their families, who are grieving the death of a loved one, share their feelings while healing themselves. They speak to each other from their hearts.

To old friends in Rastrick, Brighouse and Huddersfield, West Yorkshire.

To friends from School, College and University years who still keep in touch, and to Jean at Lea, near Preston.

To a vast wealth of friendship associated with Bolton School Girls' Division.

To all my 'Gold Stars' in the Staff Room, to Susan and Lynden the secretaries, Mary and Rose the cleaners, Chris and Shirley the nurses and Sergeant Joe.

To my two Headmistresses; Margaret Higginson, who gave me the chance of a new start in life when it was badly needed, and Margaret Spurr, who gave me the opportunities to become Senior Mistress and Examinations Officer.

To dear Sheila Stocks, who stood by me through thick and thin for many years. Not a task for the faint-hearted!

To steadfast Margaret Dickinson, who is still working her socks off and giving her all for everyone, including me.

To girls and their families who never forget.

To Mavis, Bill and Joanne Lloyd and Marjorie and Stanley Wood, all from Leigh, Lancashire.

To Barbara, Stephen, Rebecca, Stuart and Grandma Milly. May God stay close beside you and keep you safe.

To kind friends and neighbours in St Annes on Sea with their reassuring words of encouragement, and to Anne and Tom Taylor who helped to transform my flat into an 'Ideal Home'.

To Dr Kathryn Greenwood and her District Nurses.

To the doctors and nurses at Blackpool Victoria Hospital, especially my Breast Care Nurse, Gill Towers.

To warm-hearted "Mollie" in Ward 35 who gave me a birthday cake and to the other patients who sang 'Happy Birthday' round my bed.

To the cheerful nurses in the Ribblesdale Cancer Suite at the Royal Preston Hospital, who are guiding me through chemotherapy injections.

To Anthea, in Skipton, North Yorkshire, who has travelled along the same path and emerged with flying colours.

To the young assistant at Boots the Chemists Ltd., Blackpool, whose patience and optimism gave me the confidence to buy a word processor and write my book.

To my publishers, Arthur H. Stockwell Limited, who believed in me and opened the window upon a world I had never known.

Finally, to my parents who made this story possible. I visit your grave often, but not to mourn. I have let you go in peace. There is still work for me to do here on earth and life is so precious. Sometimes, when I speak to you there, with pride and gratitude, the sun suddenly appears and shines down on your grave. Who says there is no God? Oh yes, there is! Years ago, Mum, when I went through a self-centred phase, believing the world revolved around me, you were angry and said that I must learn to open up my heart. I have done my best. *Good Night and God Bless.*